Jesus' Parables of the Lost and Found

D0067469

James W. Moore

JESUS'

Parables of the Lost and Found

DIMENSIONS
FOR LIVING
NASHVILLE

JESUS' PARABLES OF THE LOST AND FOUND

Copyright © 2006 by Dimensions for Living

All rights reserved.
No part of this work may be reproduced or transmitted in any
form or by any means, electronic or mechanical, including pho-
tocopying and recording, or by any information storage or
retrieval system, except as may be expressly permitted by the
1976 Copyright Act or in writing from the publisher. Requests
for permission should be addressed in writing to Dimensions for
Living, P.O. Box 801, 201 Eighth Avenue South, Nashville, TN
37202-0801, or e-mailed to permissions@abingdonpress.com.

This book is printed on acid-free paper.

Library of Congress Cataloging-in-Publication Data

Moore, James W. (James Wendell), 1938-
   Jesus' parables of the lost and found / James W. Moore.
     p. cm.
   ISBN 0-687-49355-2 (binding: adhesive, portrait : alk. paper)
   1. Jesus Christ—Parables—Study and teaching.   I. Title.
   BT377.M66 2006
   226.8'06—dc22

                 2005029775

ISBN 13: 978-0-687-49355-5

All scripture quotations (unless noted otherwise) are taken from
the *New Revised Standard Version of the Bible,* copyright 1989,
by the Division of Christian Education of the National Council
of the Churches of Christ in the United States of America. Used
by permission. All rights reserved.

The poem "When I Say 'I Am a Christian,' " on pp. 72-73 copyright © 1988 by Carol Wimmer.

08 09 10 11 12 13 14 15—10 9 8 7 6 5 4 3 2

MANUFACTURED IN THE UNITED STATES OF AMERICA

For Sunday school teachers and Sunday school classes, with deep gratitude for letting me be a part of your class

CONTENTS

INTRODUCTION

Why did Jesus use parables, and how do we unravel them and discover their timeless and powerful messages? Let me begin by giving you five key ideas that help unlock the truths found in all the parables of Jesus.

First, Jesus spoke in parables—short stories that teach a faith lesson—to be understood and remembered, to proclaim the good news, and to make people think.

Second, Jesus saw himself as one who came to serve the needy, and he believed that the kingdom of God existed anywhere kingdom-deeds such as love, mercy, kindness, and compassion were being done.

Third, God's love for us is unconditional; and God wants us to love one another like that—unconditionally.

Fourth, one way to discover the central truth of a parable is to look for the surprise in it. Look for the moment when you lift your eyebrows, or the moment when the original hearers of the story probably thought or said in surprise—or maybe even shock—"Oh my goodness, did you hear that?"

Fifth, it's important to remember that parables are designed to convey one central truth. Parables (as opposed to allegories, in which everything in the story has a symbolic meaning) make one main point.

Parables slip up on us. They flip our values. They turn our world upside down. They surprise us. This is the great thing about the parables of Jesus: They are always relevant and always personal. They speak eloquently to you and me, here and now. In this book, we will examine six of Jesus' thought-provoking parables of the lost and found to see if we can find ourselves, and God's truth for us, in these magnificent truth-stories. They are, after all, truth-stories for us—truth-stories from the mind of Jesus that can change our lives as they proclaim God's truth for you and me.

1
The Lost and Found Sheep

Scripture: Luke 15:1-7

He called himself Father Gabriel. He was a self-proclaimed modern-day prophet of God. He came to the town where we were living in the early 1980s.

He set up shop in a storefront and pompously announced that he had special gifts from God that no other living person in the world possessed. With TV and radio spots, with billboards and newspaper ads, he proclaimed boldly that all who followed him and put their faith in him and joined his church would be blessed with great wealth and perfect health.

The *great wealth*, he said, would come

quickly to all those who joined his Father Gabriel Prosperity Plan. To ensure your place in the Prosperity Plan, all you had to do was pay $100 down and then send in $20 a week to keep you in the Prosperity Plan. When you paid your money, Father Gabriel would go into his special prayer chapel and pray for you, and then very, very soon, great wealth (out of the blue) would come into your life.

To promote his Prosperity Plan, Father Gabriel produced radio and TV spots during which people would announce that they had joined the Prosperity Plan, and then one week later, after Father Gabriel prayed for them, they had received a check for $100,000 in the mail from the estate of a distant relative; or they had gone on a quiz show and won $50,000; or they had found $75,000 buried in their own backyard.

Even though it all sounded like a hoax (and later was proved to be just that), still hundreds and hundreds of people fell for this and rushed to sign up and send in their money, prompting one cynic to say: "I don't know if the Prosperity Plan works for everybody, but it's working mighty well for Father Gabriel!"

Father Gabriel promised that all of his followers would have not only great wealth, but also *great health*. The great health would come, he said, from the special healing powers that only he possessed. With a single touch and a simple prayer, he had the power to make you well, he said. Furthermore, he announced that those who followed him would have no need of doctors or hospitals or medicines anymore, and that if any one of his members went to a doctor or took any kind of medicine (rather than coming to him), that person would be "kicked out" of his church immediately. Of course, there was a charge for the healing.

Most people in town were very suspicious of Father Gabriel and thought he was nothing more than a charlatan, a sham, "a fly-by-night, take-the-money-and-run" con man. Their suspicions proved to be right on target because two years later, Father Gabriel was arrested in another city. Weeks before, in the middle of the night, he had taken off with thousands of dollars he had bilked out of innocent, naive, gullible people. He had made off with Prosperity Plan money, with get-well-quick money, and with money people had given him to build a magnificent new church.

One of Father Gabriel's innocent victims was a member of the church I was serving at the time. Her name was Helen. Helen and her sister, Jane, were wonderful people and dedicated members of my church. They were both in their mid-sixties at the time. They were both widows, and after their husbands had died, they had moved in together to share expenses and to take care of each other.

One Sunday morning, I saw Jane in church alone. After the service, she said to me, "Jim, I'm so worried about Helen. She's gotten tied in with that Father Gabriel. I think he's a fake, but Helen can't see it. That storefront of his is just down the street from our house, and she was curious. I begged her not to go down there. I tried my best to warn her, but that Father Gabriel is a smooth talker with all those promises. He duped her and kept her coming back, and little by little she swallowed it all, hook, line, and sinker. And Jim, it breaks my heart, she went and joined that church (or whatever it is), and she's giving him all kinds of money."

Some weeks later Jane called me in a panic. "Jim, Helen fainted at work this morning. They called 911. The ambulance took her to the hospital. Her appendix was about to rupture. She's in surgery now. I got to the hospital as fast as I could. I'm really worried about her."

"I'm on my way," I said to Jane. When I got there, Jane and I prayed a prayer together, and then we waited. Soon the doctor came out. He smiled and said, "It was a close call, but she's going to be fine. The ambulance got her here just in time. Much later, and we would have lost her. The surgery went well. She will recover nicely."

"Thank God," Jane said. "Helen started having some stomach pains last week. I tried to get her to the doctor, but *no*, she went instead to that Father Gabriel. I wish he had never come to town."

Well, thankfully, the doctor was right. Helen did recover nicely and quickly, and a few days later Jane and I checked her out of the hospital and took her home. Helen was glad to see me there at the hospital, but she seemed uneasy and embarrassed in my presence. We had been in the house only a few minutes when the phone rang. Helen answered it. Shortly, she hung up and began to cry softly.

"That was Father Gabriel," she said. "He kicked me out of the church. He said I had disobeyed him and went to the hospital and relied on doctors and their medicines, and that was blatant disobedience of him and his laws.

"I tried to tell him that I passed out, that I did not call the ambulance. He told me that's no excuse, and he never, ever wants to see me again."

Helen cried some more. Jane and I hugged her, and at the same time we said, "Helen, forget about him, come on back to our church. Come on back home."

Helen looked right into my eyes and said, "Jim, I'm so ashamed. I'm so embarrassed. How could I have been so foolish and so gullible? I want to come back to our church, but I don't know how the people at the church feel about me now or how they will treat me after what I've done and after the silly way I have acted."

I said, "Helen, they will treat you like you have never been away."

But, actually, I understated it! The very next Sunday, the people of our church did even better! They treated her like the guest of honor at a great homecoming celebration. They hugged her and kissed her and patted her and complimented her. They acted like they had waited all year long for just this moment, to say with joy and thanksgiving and relief, "Welcome home, Helen!"

You know where the people learned that sort of compassion, don't you? They learned it at church, at Sunday school. They learned it from Jesus. They learned it from Jesus' parable of the lost sheep in Luke 15.

Like the lost sheep, Helen had just wandered

off, just drifted away, and when she was found and brought home, there was a great sigh of relief, a great prayer of thanksgiving, and a great celebration because this beloved and precious sheep was lost, and now she was found and was safely back with the flock.

In Luke 15, Jesus is painting his best picture of what God is like and what God wants us to be like. In this parable, Jesus is dramatically showing us three great things about God and his love.

Let's take a look at each of these.

First of All, God's Love Is Inclusive, and God Wants Us to Be Inclusive in Our Loving

The Good Shepherd wants all of his sheep to be in the flock, even those who wander off. He can't rest until all the sheep are safely accounted for and safely included. His love is inclusive, and he wants us to live daily in that spirit. He wants us to be inclusive also.

Fred Craddock tells about how some years ago he used to go home to West Tennessee for Christmas. Each year was pretty much the same. He would go back to the town where he grew up, and he would always stop by a restaurant to visit one of his old high school buddies named Buck who owned the restaurant. Buck was always glad to see Fred, and he would give Fred a cup of coffee and a piece of chess pie for free.

But one year it was different. Buck asked Fred to go with him to a different place for coffee. Fred thought it was strange to go to somebody else's restaurant, but he sensed that Buck was thinking deep thoughts and wanted to talk. They sipped their coffee, and then suddenly Buck said to Fred, "The curtain has to come down."

The curtain Buck was referring to was the curtain in his restaurant that separated the black patrons from the white patrons. Buck's restaurant was like other buildings in the little town, a long "shotgun" building with a front entrance off the street and a back entrance off the alley behind the restaurant. The white diners came in off the street, and the black diners entered from the back alley. A curtain across the center of the building separated the black diners from the white. It had always been that way; but now Buck was saying, "The curtain has to come down." And as Fred Craddock tells it, this conversation between these two old friends took place.

I said, "Good, bring it down."

[Buck] said, "That's easy for you to say. Come in here from out of state and tell me how to run my business."

I said, "Okay, leave it up."

Buck said, "I can't leave it up."

I said, "Then, take it down."

"I can't take it down!" [Buck's] in terrible shape. After a while Buck said, "If I take that curtain down, I lose a lot of my customers. If I leave that curtain up, I lose my soul."(Fred Craddock, *Craddock Stories*, ed. Mike Graves and Richard F. Ward [St. Louis, Mo.: Chalice Press, 2001], 61.)

Thankfully we live in a different era today. But let me ask you something: Do you grapple with a similar ethical dilemma of your own? Do you have "curtains" in your life, curtains that separate and divide people? curtains that shut people out? curtains that hurt and shun and exclude other human beings? curtains that promote and perpetuate prejudice and discrimination or bigotry? curtains that poison your soul?

The parable of the lost sheep was told by Jesus to show us how loving and inclusive God is and to remind us that there are no "curtains that separate" in God's flock. All are valued. All are cherished. All are treasured. All are wanted. All are welcomed. All are included. That's the way God is, and that's the way God wants us to be. God's love is inclusive, and God wants us to be inclusive in our loving. That's number one.

Second, God's Love Is Forgiving, and God Wants Us to Be Forgiving in Our Loving

The lost sheep wandered off, and yet the Good Shepherd cared for him and went looking for him and found him and brought him safely back home. That's what God's love is like. Jesus tells us in this parable that God is always ready to forgive, eager to forgive, quick to forgive and that God wants us to live like that, to emulate his forgiving spirit.

Some years ago, I met an older woman who had a really beautiful spirit of forgiveness. She was an inspiration to everyone who knew her. One day I asked her about her gracious spirit of forgiveness. She smiled and told me that many years before, when she was a teenager, she had gotten into serious trouble. She was scared to death and didn't know what to do. She finally got up the nerve to tell her parents what she had done. She thought they might kick her out of the house and disown her; but to the contrary, they loved her more than ever. They supported her and encouraged her and loved her through that most difficult situation, and, the woman said, "They forgave me!" Their gracious forgiveness meant so much to her. Their merciful, compassionate spirit touched her deep in her soul, and this woman made a vow then and there to be a forgiving person like her parents were. She said, "Because of them and what they did for me, I have dedicated my life to the spirit of forgiveness."

As Christians, that is our calling. We have been forgiven so much by the Christ of the cross. How could we *not* be forgiving?

If you ever wonder, *Should I forgive that person who has hurt me or wronged me or betrayed me?* just remember Jesus on the cross saying, "Father, forgive them." That's the measuring stick for forgiveness.

In his life, death, and resurrection, and also in his teaching, Jesus shows us that God's love is inclusive and that God's love is forgiving and that God wants us to be inclusive and forgiving like him.

Third and Finally, God's Love Is Sacrificial, and God Wants Us to Be Sacrificial in Our Loving

One of my favorite stories is the one about the young professional baseball player some years ago who prided himself on being a great hitter. He knew he could make it big in the major leagues if he could just get his chance.

For several years, he bounced around in the minor leagues. Then one year toward the end of the season, the major league parent team brought him up to help them as they were in the thick of a heated pennant race.

Finally, this was his chance. But he was promptly put on the bench! Day after day went by as the rookie was itching to bat, to show what he could do, to show the world that he was a great hitter—and still he sat on the bench.

Then one day the manager called for the rookie to pinch hit. This was the dramatic moment he had dreamed of for so long—a crucial game, the last inning, the score tied, and a runner on first base. The rookie's heart pounded with excitement as he stepped into the batter's box. Routinely he glanced down toward the third-base coach—and he could not believe his eyes: They were giving him the signal to sacrifice! Here was his chance to show the world his greatness as a hitter, and the coaches were telling him to bunt, to make an out on purpose to advance the runner to second base.

The rookie ignored the signal, took three hefty swings, and struck out. When he returned to the dugout, he was met by a red-faced, irate manager. "Son, what's the matter with you? Didn't you see the signal to sacrifice?" "Yes sir, I saw it," said the rookie, "but I didn't think you *meant* it!"

"I saw it, but I didn't think you meant it!" Isn't that what we say to God? On page after page of the Scriptures, God says to us, "Sacrifice! Sacrifice! Love others! Lay down your life for others! Sacrifice yourself for the good of the team! Lose yourself! Be self-giving!"

That's what God says to us. That is God's signal to us. But we are not so sure that he means it. Well, God showed us he meant it on a cross!

The point is clear and obvious. In words and deeds, in parables and actions, Jesus taught us that God is the Good Shepherd who lays his life on the line with love to include and to forgive and to save his sheep, and that God wants us to be inclusive, forgiving, and sacrificial like that in our loving and in our living.

2
The Lost and Found Coin

Scripture: Luke 15:8-10

Some time ago, ABC's *Nightline* presented a powerful and amazing true story about the redemption of a notorious drug addict who had been lost and then found. The program was entitled "The Doctor and the Reverend."

"The Doctor" was an African American man who was well known and much feared in one of the roughest and toughest sections in the United States, the Badlands of Philadelphia, a run-down inner-city neighborhood infested with drug addicts of all ages and drug deals of the most dangerous kind. This man was called "The Doctor" because he had been doing drugs and dealing drugs and shooting up heroin himself and in others for thirty-five years.

He had been thrust out onto the streets of Philadelphia when he was only thirteen years old, and he had been a drug addict and a pusher all those years. Although "The Doctor" was his nickname, in the Badlands of Philadelphia he was also known as "Seville" because of his habit of stealing Cadillac Sevilles and then selling them quickly to produce "ready cash" to support his drug habit and his drug business.

Seville, "The Doctor," was a rough, tough, hard, and hostile character, and when he walked by, people backed away to give him plenty of space. But then something amazing happened that changed everything and turned his life completely around.

A young minister decided to do something no one else wanted to do—to go serve God in the Badlands of Philadelphia. She had wanted to be a missionary to Africa, but she got married and had five children, and that door of opportunity to serve in Africa never opened for her. So, she decided to become a missionary in Philadelphia's harshest inner-city region, the Badlands.

It's noteworthy that she would undertake such a faith venture in such a dangerous place.

She was an attractive young woman, and we can only imagine the horrible things that could have happened to her there. But in faith she went, and the very first day she did a very courageous thing. She stopped a drug addict on the street and asked him: "Who's the 'baddest of the bad' in the Badlands?"

The addict answered: "That would be Seville, The Doctor. No question about it, he's the baddest of the bad down here, but if you go near him, you be careful."

She got directions on where to find him, and boldly she went. She told Seville who she was and what she wanted to do, and how, in the spirit of Jesus Christ, she just wanted to help people find a better life. Seville was impressed with her and fascinated by her courage, her faith, and her servant spirit, so he put out an order in the Badlands that everyone was to treat her, The Reverend, with respect, and no one was to mess with her.

So, the young woman began her ministry there and over time became a very beloved and respected person in the inner city. As Seville watched her work and as he got to know her better, his heart began to soften; and through this minister, he realized that he wanted a better life and that God was his only hope.

So he turned to God. He went into rehab, and with the help of God and by the power of God's amazing grace, he became a new man!

He no longer has anything to do with drugs.

He no longer injects others with drugs either.

He has been made clean and whole.

He has been totally converted.

He is an absolutely different human being.

He is a new person in Christ.

The TV news correspondent who was interviewing The Doctor and The Reverend asked Seville if he could put his finger on what was the one factor that caused his miraculous turnaround. Without hesitation, Seville replied: "Jesus Christ." The TV journalist pushed on: "Yes, I know," he said, "but tell me more. Aside from that, what other factors were involved?" Seville only smiled and said, "There are no other factors, my friend. There's just one factor. His name is Jesus Christ."

For thirty-seven of his fifty years, Seville had been lost in drugs, lost in crime, lost in addiction, lost in the sins so prevalent in that kind of existence, and then out of the blue, here came God looking for him in the missionary heart of a young minister who showed up one day in the Badlands of Philadelphia, Pennsylvania.

Seville was lost, and then, thank God, he was

found. That's what this parable of the lost coin is really all about—being sadly lost and then joyously found. In Luke 15 we find, back to back to back, *three* great parables about being lost and found, and each one shows a different way people can get lost in our world.

First, the parable of the lost sheep shows us how people (like lost sheep) can get lost by just wandering off, just drifting away.

Second, the parable of the lost coin reminds us that sometimes people can get lost through no fault of their own. They can get lost because of the actions of someone else.

Third, the parable of the lost son (which we will look at in chapter 3) depicts how people sometimes willfully and rebelliously and arrogantly just run off and get lost in the far country by their own selfish choosing.

But in Luke 15, in all three cases, the lost are found and brought home and are restored to their proper place in the family.

In this chapter, we want to take a closer look at the parable of the lost coin. How did the coin get lost? Why was there such urgency to find it? And why was there such joy at the end when the lost coin was finally discovered?

Losing a coin in a Palestinian peasant home would not be a difficult thing to do, because the houses were dark. There were no picture windows, no sky lights, no light bulbs, just one small circular window only twelve to eighteen inches across. Consequently, not much sunlight could come in. In addition, there were no hardwood floors. The floor was packed-down dirt covered with dried reeds and rushes. So to look for a coin lost on the floor was indeed like looking for a needle in a haystack.

Dr. William Barclay, in his *Daily Bible Study Series* commentary on Luke, suggests that there were two possible reasons why the woman was so eager and anxious to find the coin. For one thing, the single coin does not sound like much money to us, but it was more than a day's wage back then, and most of the people were quite poor. But then, Barclay also points out:

> There may have been a much more romantic reason. The mark of a married woman was a head-dress made of ten silver coins linked together by a silver chain. For years maybe a girl would scrape and save to amass her ten coins, for the head-dress was almost the equivalent of her wedding ring. . . . It may well be that it was one of these coins that the woman had lost, and so she searched for

it as urgently as any woman would search if she lost her marriage ring. (William Barclay, *Daily Bible Study Series, The Gospel of Luke*, rev. ed. [Philadelphia: Westminster Press, 1975], 202)

And then, imagine her joy when she finds it. In this parable, Jesus is reminding us that God loves and values and cherishes and prizes and treasures each one of us like that. When we get lost, he urgently wants to seek us and find us; and when he does find us, there is great joy and relief in his heart and in his kingdom.

Now, what makes this parable unique and different from the other two (in Luke 15) is that the coin gets lost through no fault of its own. It doesn't wander off like the lost sheep. It doesn't run away like the lost son. No, it gets lost because somebody else drops it, somebody else loses it, somebody else lets it get away. There is a sermon there somewhere, and it's a sermon about our awesome responsibility not to lose the "coins" that are so precious to us and to God.

Let me show you what I mean by breaking this down. Look with me at three places where we have a keen responsibility not to lose the coins that are so valuable and so important and so precious.

First of All, this Parable Underscores the Keen Responsibility We Have for Our Children

There is no "coin" more precious than our children. It's our great responsibility as Christian families to keep them in the circle of our love and God's love, to keep them in the family, to keep them from getting lost.

Earlier, I told you the story of Seville, who got lost and became "the baddest of the bad" in the Badlands of Philadelphia. How did that happen? How did he end up out on the inner-city streets at such a young age? It was probably not his fault at first. Somebody dropped the ball. Somebody let him get lost in a world he wasn't ready for or prepared for. He was launched in the wrong direction. He was pushed out into the world to survive on his own at too early an age, and he got lost in a world of drugs and crime and darkness.

Have you heard the story about the pastor who looked out of his study window and saw that a little kitten had climbed high up into a skinny tree in his backyard? The kitten was trembling with fear and was afraid to come down. The pastor went out and tried to coax the kitten down with warm milk and food, but no luck. The kitten would not budge.

The tree was not sturdy enough to climb, so the pastor decided to tie one end of a rope to the tree and the other end to the bumper of his car, and then to drive away just enough to bend the tree over far enough to where he could reach the cat.

The plan was working beautifully. The tree was bending over nicely; just a little more and he could have saved the kitten. But then, oh my goodness, the rope broke! The tree went *boing!* and the kitten instantly sailed through the air and out of sight! (Now, let me hurry to tell you this is going to turn out all right.)

The pastor felt terrible. He searched all over the neighborhood, but no one had seen a stray kitten. So, he prayed, *Lord, I don't know what else to do but to commit this little kitten into your keeping.*

A few days later, the pastor was in the grocery store, where he saw one of his church members and noticed that she had cat food in her grocery cart. "Oh," he said. "I see you have some cat food. Do you have a new cat?"

The woman answered, "You won't believe this." She proceeded to tell how her daughter had been begging for a cat, but she kept refusing. The woman finally told her daughter, "I'll tell you what. You pray about it, and if God gives you a cat, I'll let you keep it." She told the pastor, "I watched my daughter go out into the backyard, get on her knees, and ask God for a cat. And really, Pastor, you won't believe this, but I saw it with my own eyes: A kitten suddenly came flying out of the blue sky with its paws outspread and landed right in front of her! So, now we have a new kitten. We named him Matthew, which as you know means 'Gift from God.'"

Now, that's a funny story to me, but let me take it to a deeper and more serious level. Whether we realize it or not, we are launching our children and youth out into the world. And before we launch them into high school and college and life on their own, we had better be sure that they are ready—that they have the roots and wings and faith they will need for the living of these days.

Let me say something to parents and grandparents and older brothers and sisters and teachers and indeed to all of us, with all the feeling I have in my heart. You can give your children a digital camera, a DVD player, a state-of-the-art cell phone, or an expensive automobile if you want to. But let me tell you something: Without question, the best gift you can give them is Jesus Christ. If you want to do something good for your children, if you want to give them the gift that keeps on giving, the gift that will keep them from getting lost, then introduce them to Jesus Christ! Get them completely involved in his church. Show them how important your faith is to you. Help them discover the power and the light of the Christian faith!

Let me hurry to put in this quick thought. I know of situations in which the family did everything right, and the child still went off and got lost. That does happen, and when it does, it breaks our hearts. But most of the time, children—as they grow up and become adults—hold onto and treasure the values, principles, and faith they learned at home.

So, that's number one. The parable of the lost coin underscores the keen responsibility we have for our children, to prepare them lovingly and diligently so they won't get lost.

Second, this Parable Underscores the Keen Responsibility We Have for Our Church

As followers of Christ and as members of his church, we have a keen responsibility to live constantly in the Spirit of Christ and to represent him and his church well so that we don't cause others to get lost.

Every Sunday (indeed, every day) people come to our church, and the way we treat them, the way we respond to them, the way we speak to them, the way we relate to them determines whether or not they will ever come back. What an awesome responsibility we have as Christians and as church members!

Sometimes I wonder about this (a haunting question): Is there anybody, anywhere in the world today, who is not in the church because of *me*? Have I ever said something or done something or failed to do something that drove somebody away from the church?

Or, on the other side of the coin, I wonder if there is anybody, anywhere in the world today, who is *in* the church because of me. Have I ever said something or done something or touched someone in a positive way that brought that person to Christ and into Christ's church?

We have a wonderful young woman and her two beautiful daughters in our church today because of one of our ushers. The young woman had just gone through a painful divorce. She had been depressed for some weeks, but she knew she needed to be in church and to have her girls in Sunday school and church. So, she made up her mind to attend church somewhere the very next Sunday. She chose to come to St. Luke's to give us a try.

She came and parked in one of our visitors' parking spots, and just as she turned off the engine, it started pouring down rain! There she was with two preschool children and no umbrella. The woman thought, *It's no use. There's no way I can get into the church with these two girls without getting us all soaking wet. I guess we'll just go back home and forget it.*

But just then, she heard a gentle knocking on her car window. One of our ushers had run to help her with two umbrellas. He took one girl and one umbrella, and the woman took the other girl and the other umbrella, and they got into the church and they stayed. And now, they have become one of the finest families in our church, not because of the sermon I preached that day, but because one of our ushers saw their need and rushed out to help them in a simple but profound way.

What if this usher hadn't done that? That family might have driven away and never come back, and three precious coins of God could have been lost. The parable of the lost and found coin reminds us that we have a keen responsibility, first, for our children, and second, for our church.

Third and Finally, this Parable Underscores the Keen Responsibility We Have for Our Friends

There's an old story about a college student who became a Christian and joined the church in springtime. Shortly after, he went up North to work in a logging camp for the summer. His friends at church were worried about him, a new Christian being exposed to the tough life of the logging camp. They were afraid that the rough, worldly lumberjacks might tease him harshly or even persecute him because of his faith, or even worse, that they might tempt him to shortcut his best self. These friends prayed for him daily.

When the summer ended and the student returned home, his friends at church quizzed him: "Did you make it all right?" "Was it difficult?" "Did those lumberjacks give you a hard time because of your faith?"

The young man answered, "I made it fine. No problems at all; they never found out that I'm a Christian!"

Let me ask you something.

Can people tell that you are a Christian?

Do your friends and coworkers know that you are a Christian?

Do you stand out in a crowd because the spirit of Christ is radiant in you?

Or do you just blend in?

As Christians, we have a keen responsibility for our children, for our church, and for our friends to live our faith daily and to help others see the light of Christ in us. You don't have to wear a sign or get up on a soapbox or preach on a street corner. Just live your faith daily and celebrate God's amazing grace, because once you were lost, and now you are found.

3

The Lost and Found Son

Scripture: Luke 15:11-32

We have a young man in our church family who is in the military. He is now on his second tour of duty in Iraq. Every now and then I drive down the street where his mom and dad live here in Houston, and I'm always touched to see that they have yellow ribbons on all of the trees in their front yard.

The yellow ribbon is a dramatic part of our culture now. It means:

"We love you!"

"We miss you!"

"You are wanted and treasured and welcome here!"

"Please hurry home!"

The yellow ribbon is a powerful and eloquent symbol for the sentiment, "You are loved and wanted and welcome here," but where in the world did that idea come from? Well, probably from a hit recording made some years ago by Tony Orlando.

In 1973, Tony Orlando and Dawn recorded the song "Tie a Yellow Ribbon 'Round the Old Oak Tree." It became the number-one hit record for the year, it became Tony Orlando's theme song, and it grew into an American anthem of hope and homecoming, reunion and renewal. We have used this song (and its yellow ribbon symbol) to welcome home soldiers, POWs, hostages, and lost children.

As you listen to the words of the song, you get the picture of a young man who has run away from his wife (or girlfriend) and has been gone for three long years; perhaps he has been in prison. Now he has come to his senses and wants to come home, but he doesn't know what kind of reception awaits him there.

After the hurt and heartache he has caused, he doesn't know how welcome he will be, so he has sent a message ahead to his girlfriend, saying, in effect, "If you still love me, if you forgive me, if you still want me, then tie a yellow

ribbon around the old oak tree. If I see the ribbon, I'll get off the bus; if not, I'll stay on the
bus and stay out of your life."

Now, I have a strong suspicion that this song
draws at least some of its inspiration from an
old, old story that preachers have loved to tell
for many generations. There are such obvious
similarities that it just couldn't be a coinci-
dence. See what you think.

The sermonic story takes place on a train
rather than on a bus.

The young man has run away from his family rather than from a girlfriend.

The tree is a crabapple tree rather than an old
oak tree.

And a white rag is used rather than a yellow
ribbon.

Except for those minor differences, the
preacher story is almost identical to the pop
song. The story goes like this. A young man is
on a train. He seems deeply troubled—nervous,
anxious, afraid, fighting back the tears. An
older man seated beside him senses that something is wrong, and he asks the younger man if
he is all right. The young man, needing to talk,
blurts out his story.

Three years before, after an argument with
his father one evening, the young man ran

away from home. He had chased back and forth across the country looking for freedom and happiness, and with every passing day he had become more miserable. Finally it dawned on him that more than anything, he wanted to go home. Home was where he wanted to be, but he didn't know how his parents felt about him now. After all, he had hurt them deeply. He had said some cruel, callous things to his father. He had left an arrogant note on his pillow for his parents to find. He wouldn't blame them if they never wanted to see him again.

The young man had written ahead to his parents to say that he would be passing by their backyard on the afternoon train on a particular day, and if they forgave him, if they wanted to see him, if they wanted him to come home, they could tie a white rag on the crabapple tree in the backyard. If the white rag was there, he would get off the train and come home; if not, he would stay on the train and stay out of their lives forever.

Just as the young man finished his story, the train began to slow down as it pulled into the town where his family lived. Tension was heavy, so much so that the young man couldn't bear to look. The older man said, "I'll watch for you. You put your head down and relax. Just close your eyes. I'll watch for you."

As they came to the old home place, the older man looked and then touched the young man excitedly on the shoulder and said, "Look, son, look! You can go home! You can go home! There's a white rag on every limb!"

Isn't that a great story? The truth is, that powerful story is simply a modern retelling of the greatest short story in history, namely, Jesus' parable of the lost son. That preacher story was probably inspired by this parable.

The parable of the lost son in Luke 15—which is commonly rcfcrred to as the parable of the prodigal son—is not well named, because actually the parable is about a father and *two* sons. And besides that, the father is the real hero in this story, not the prodigal son. In the father we see the central truth Jesus wanted to communicate through the story. It probably should be called the parable of the loving father.

Justifiably, it has been called the greatest short story in the world because it is packed with the stuff of life. It has everything.

There are powerful symbols here—the robe, the ring, the sandals, the inheritance, the feast, the pigs, the far country.

There is provocative drama here, the fascinating interplay of emotions—love and jealousy, tenderness and rebellion, acceptance and rejection, compassion and envy, humility and arrogance.

There is deep theological understanding here—the picture of sin, penitence, reconciliation, redemption, grace, and forgiveness.

All of that is here, and more. Most important, though, we have here the picture of how Jesus saw God, the picture of how Jesus understood God to be.

If Jesus had been a painter and had painted a picture of God, it's likely he would have painted God boldly and tenderly as a loving father. Hold that image in your mind for a moment. We are going to come back to that, but first remember the parable with me.

One day Jesus told the story about a man who had two sons. The younger son grew restless and came to his father with a brash demand: "Give me my share of the property! Give me my inheritance now!" In effect, he was saying, "I don't want to wait around till you die. Let me have my inheritance now!" So the father divided his property between his two sons—two-thirds to the elder brother and one-third to the younger son.

A few days later, the younger son turned his property into cash and went off into the far country, where he promptly spent every penny. He squandered his money in "dissolute living," which brings all kinds of images to mind, doesn't it?

All of his money gone and very hungry, the younger son took a job as a feeder of pigs. A feeder of pigs; this job was considered to be the pits, the depths of degradation for a young Jewish man. Now, according to the story, the young man was so hungry that even the pods eaten by the pigs looked good to him.

There the young man "came to himself." He realized that the place for him was not in the pigsty, but the real place for him was at home with his father and his brother. So, he said, "I will arise and go to my father, and I will say to him, 'Father, I have sinned against heaven and before you. I am so ashamed. I am no longer worthy to be called your son. Just let me be one of your hired servants" (Luke 15:18-19, paraphrased). Remember that a "hired servant" was the lowest servant. The ordinary servant was like a member of the family, but the hired servant was only a day laborer who could be dismissed at a moment's notice.

The prodigal son left the far country and headed for home. You can just see him trudging, rehearsing his confession over and over.

39

Now, notice this. When the younger son drew near home, his father saw him, and the father's heart went out to him, and the father ran down the road to meet his son. The father hugged him and kissed him. And don't miss this: The father interrupted his son's confession; he doesn't want to hear it. He only wants to get on with the celebration. He wants to have a party! He shouts, "Quickly, bring the best robe and put it on him! [The robe symbolized that the returned prodigal was the guest of honor.] Put a ring on his hand! [The ring was the symbol of authority, like the power of attorney for the family.] Put sandals on his feet! [The sandals meant sonship; the master's children wore shoes, while the servant's children went barefoot.] Prepare the fatted calf, and let us eat and make merry; for this my son was dead, and now he is alive again. He was lost, and now he is found!"

And so they had a great party, and lived happily ever after. End of story? No! Not quite, because the prodigal son has an elder brother.

As the prodigal son was returning home to a celebratory greeting, the elder brother was doing what all elder brothers ought to do—he was in the field, dutifully at work, doing the chores. When the elder brother heard music at the house, he asked, "What's going on?" A servant answered, "Your brother has returned home, and your father is so happy that he has killed the fatted calf and called for a great celebration." Now, this didn't set well with the elder brother. He was angry, and he refused to go in.

The father came out to explain and to encourage him to come and join the party. But the elder brother felt rejected and slighted, and out of his hurt and resentment, he replied bitterly, "Listen! These many years I have served you and I never disobeyed your command; yet you never even gave me a young goat that I might make merry and have a feast with my friends. But when this s*on of yours* [emphasis added; sounds almost like a curse, doesn't it?], came who has devoured your property with harlots, you killed for him the fatted calf."

The father tried to reason with him, "But, son, you are always with me, and all that is mine is yours. It was fitting to make merry and be glad, for this, your brother, was dead and is alive again. He was lost, and now is found" (Luke 15:29-32, paraphrased).

What a powerful parable this is! Packed with meaning, packed with life! Now, we could go off in lots of different directions in trying to understand what it's about—and in fact, we will be examining this parable in different ways in chapters 4 and 5 as well. But for now, I want us to zero in quickly on the fascinating characters here, to do some character sketches.

Look First at the Prodigal Son

When you look at him, the descriptive adjectives fly fast and furious: *rebellious, restless, discontent, ruthless, arrogant, prideful, immature, selfish, egotistical!* But, you see, all of these are symptoms of something deeper. What is his sin? Simply this: Even though he is a son, he doesn't want to be a son; and even though he is a brother, he doesn't want to be a brother.

The prodigal son rejects his father, and he rejects his brother. And anytime you do that, you are in the far country—far from what God intended—for God meant us to be children to him and brothers and sisters to one another.

It's hard to remember this, because we want to be Number One. Remember Bishop Gerald Kennedy's story about the young man proposing to his girlfriend. The young man said, "I'm not wealthy like Jerome. I don't have expensive tastes like Jerome. I don't have a country estate like Jerome. I'm not handsome like Jerome.

But, my darling, I love you." To which his girl-friend replied, "I love you too, but tell me more about Jerome!"

We go through life saying, in effect, "What's in it for me? Tell me more about Jerome." This was the prodigal son's problem. He didn't want to answer to his father. And notice this: When you run away from your father, you are also deserting your brother!

Look next at ...

The Elder Brother

Again, the descriptive adjectives fly: *resentful, judgmental, envious, jealous, hostile, bitter, angry, self-righteous.* But again, these are symptoms of something deeper! What is his sin? It is simply the same as that of the prodigal son, except turned around and more subtle. Even though he is a brother, he doesn't want to be a brother. Even though he is a son, he doesn't want to be a son. He rejects his brother, and in so doing he rejects his father; when he runs out on his brother, in the same motion he deserts his father.

The best way to love God is to love God's children. The way we hurt God most is when we are cruel or hurtful to any of God's children.

If the prodigal son committed the seven deadly sins, then the elder brother committed the seven deadly virtues—and each of the two men, in his own way, rejected childhood and brotherhood.

This brings us to the main character, the real hero of the story.

The Father

Again in this dramatic story, the descriptive adjectives fly fast and furious! The father is *gracious, merciful, big-spirited, magnanimous, forgiving, compassionate, patient, and loving*. And here is the key. This is how Jesus pictured God—not as a harsh, vindictive judge; not as an impersonal, uncaring computer—but as a gracious, loving father.

Now, a parable is a story that is designed to make one central point, and the point of this parable is found not in the revelry of the prodigal son, and not in the bitterness of the elder brother. The point of this parable is found in the goodness of the father, the forgiveness of the father; it is found in the father's amazing grace.

The message here is "good news." The message here is that God prizes and values and treasures all of his children.

The father wants both of his sons to come to the party, to join the celebration, to feast at his table. The Father wants all of his children to come hand-in-hand to his supper.

Some years ago, a young woman came to see me. She had done something wrong. She knew it. She admitted it. She was penitent but haunted by one question. She said: "How can I know that God will forgive me for what I have done?"

I answered, "You can know it because Jesus told us that God is like a loving parent who is anxious to love, quick to forgive, and eager to reconcile." To drive the point home, I said to her, "What if I were your father and you told me your story, just as you told it a moment ago? I would have two choices. One option would be that I could say, 'Get out of my sight. You have dishonored our family. I don't ever want to see you again.' Or a second option would be that I could say, 'I'm so sorry this has happened to you. I love you so much. Let me help you make a new start with your life.'"

I paused for a moment, and then I said, "Which of those two things do you think I would do?"

The young woman answered, "The second one."

"Why?" I asked.

"Because," she said, "you are a father, and I know you love your children."

"Precisely!" I said, "And if *I'm* capable of that kind of forgiveness, how much more is our Father God!"

Now, let me ask you something, a very personal question: How are things with you?

Have you been squandering away your life in the far country?

Have you been running away from your Father and your brothers and sisters?

Have you been "shortcutting" your best self?

Do you want to come home?

Well, you can! The Father is waiting—waiting just for you. He is running down the road to meet you with open arms! And, look at that: On the gate of his home place is a great big yellow ribbon!

4

The Lost and Found Gifts

Scripture: Luke 15:11-24

It happened on June 29, 2004, on American Airlines Flight 866. Twelve U.S. soldiers coming home from Iraq were scheduled to fly on that plane from Atlanta to Chicago. When the first of those soldiers boarded the plane, a businessman suddenly stood up, shook his hand, and said, "What's your seat number, soldier?" "It's 23B, sir," said the soldier. "No, son," said the businessman, "that's *my* seat. Here's *your* seat, in first class!" The businessman handed the surprised young soldier his first-class boarding pass, took the soldier's 23B boarding pass, pointed the young soldier to the first-class seat, and then walked back and sat down in seat 23B.

The other passengers in first class were so touched by the businessman's gracious gesture, that they all did the same thing, and all twelve of the young soldiers just home from harm's way in Iraq ended up sitting in first class!

Word quickly spread throughout the plane about what had happened, and suddenly the flight from Atlanta to Chicago became different. It took on a happy, fun, celebrative party atmosphere. The soldiers were so touched and so humble and so thankful. They spent the entire flight saying "thank you"—but really, what was happening was a spontaneous, spur of the moment opportunity for the other passengers to say "thank you" and "welcome home" to the young soldiers, prompting one of the flight attendants to say, "If nothing else, those young soldiers got a great homecoming."

Speaking of a great homecoming, that is precisely what we see in the parable of the prodigal son in Luke 15, which some have called the greatest homecoming story of all time. In this powerful parable (which we began to examine in chapter 3), Jesus is showing us two very important things: first, what God is like; and second, what God wants *us* to be like, and in both instances, the word is *grace*. In the story, the father is gracious, and he wants his children to be gracious like him.

Remember the story with me. A man had two sons. The younger son gets restless, demands his inheritance early, converts it into cash, and arrogantly heads out for the far country to be his own boss and to do his own thing. He squanders his money, loses everything, falls on hard times, sees the error and selfishness of his ways, is penitent and remorseful and ashamed, and decides to return home. Earlier he had left in arrogance. And now, he returns in humility, wanting and needing forgiveness, but knowing that he doesn't deserve it.

The father sees him coming. We get the feeling that the father has looked hopefully down that road a thousand times. The father runs to greet the lost son and to welcome him home. The father is so overjoyed that he calls for a great feast to receive the prodigal home in a celebrative way, and to include him again in the family circle. So, they have a big party.

The prodigal son's elder brother doesn't like this one bit. He is jealous, angry, resentful, and he refuses to go in, he refuses to participate, and in the process he makes himself look bad. His pettiness is exposed in all of its ugliness when it's placed alongside the brilliant light of the father's loving, forgiving spirit, the father's amazing grace.

The point is clear: God is full of grace, like that father. God is gracious like that father, and God wants his children—he wants us—to be gracious too. God gives us his amazing grace, and he wants us to live in that spirit. God wants us to be gracious and forgiving and loving, like him.

This all becomes even more clear when we focus on the gifts the loving father gave to his son that day, gifts that were lost to the prodigal son but then found again upon his welcome return home; three incredible gifts that are also the gifts God wants to give to each one of us, three amazing gifts: the robe, the ring, and the shoes. These great gifts remind us that God is loving and gracious, and God wants us to be loving and gracious like him.

Let's take a look together at God's great gifts.

First of All, There Is the Robe—the Best Robe, the Robe Reserved for a VIP Guest of Honor

The key to finding the main point of a parable is to look for the surprise in it. The surprise for the listeners who first heard Jesus tell this story was the unconditional love of the father. When Jesus came to the point in the story that describes the younger son's homecoming, that first-century audience fully expected the father either to reject the prodigal son altogether, or at best to put strong conditions on the son's return to the family. Those early listeners expected the father to say, "I don't know you!" "You are dead to me!" "You are not my son!" "You are not part of this family anymore!" Or, at least, to say, "Well, you can come back on probation," or "You can be one of my hired hands, but not my *son*, until you have met certain conditions."

Even the prodigal himself expected to hear that! Remember his confession: "Father, I am no longer worthy to be called your son; treat me like one of your hired servants." You can just picture in your mind the image of those first-century listeners, rubbing their hands together at this point in the story and saying, "Boy, oh boy, is that prodigal son going to get it now! His father is going to rip into him and set him straight!"

Imagine their surprise, their disbelief, their shock, when they heard Jesus say instead that the father, with joy and relief and love and

gratitude, ran down the road to meet his returning son with open arms. With his robes flapping
in the wind, the father couldn't wait to get to
his boy. He ran to welcome his son home and
to love him back into the family.

Some of those people in that first-century
audience may have fainted on the spot! Some of
them probably grumbled about this new-
fangled idea. They were not expecting this.
They were not expecting the father's unconditional love.

And on top of that, not only did the father
run to meet his returning son, not only did the
father welcome him home warmly, not only
did the father forgive him immediately, but—
can you believe it?—the father placed upon him
the best robe, the robe that was saved for very,
very special occasions, the robe that was saved
for a very, very special guest of honor such as
the mayor or the governor or the high priest.

But here comes this wayward son home,
bankrupt, hungry, dirty, broken, disheveled,
full of shame and guilt and remorse, shoulders
slumped in embarrassment and defeat, and of
all things—surprise of surprises—the father
gives him the best robe and treats him like a
VIP guest of honor.

One Sunday morning some years ago, a

young woman joined our church. After the service, I was visiting with her. I said to her, "Have you been visiting our church for some time?" "No," she said, "you may find this hard to believe, but today was the first time I ever set foot in this church, and I want to tell you what happened to me today."

The woman said, "I've had a rough life, lots of hard knocks, and I had become blasé and somewhat bitter. But I knew I had to try to do better, so I decided to give it one last chance in this church." She said, "I came in this morning pretty cynical. My attitude was to test you, to see if anybody in this big church would notice me or speak to me. I didn't really think anybody would, but was I ever wrong about that!

"As soon as I stepped inside the door, this cute, vivacious, energetic woman ran over to greet me and welcome me. She wasn't big in stature, but she had such a huge personality, and she was so wonderful! Immediately she hugged me and took me under her wing. She treated me like I was the Queen of England and she had been waiting all year long just for this moment to reach out to me. She was so radiant! She had to be in her late eighties, but she was so full of life and so proud of her church. She took me to her Sunday school class and introduced me to everybody as if I were a celebrity. She took me to church and introduced me to every person we saw. She made me feel like the guest of honor today. And I thought to myself, *If that's what this church is like, then I want to be a part of it,* so I just came down and joined!"

The young woman paused for a moment, and then she said, "But now I'm so embarrassed because I can't remember that wonderful woman's name." "Was it Dorothy Coffee?" I asked. "That's it!" she said with excitement, and then she asked, "How many members are in this church?" I said, "About 7,500." And the young woman said, "Out of 7,500 members, how did you know I was talking about Dorothy Coffee?" And I answered, "We have 7,500 members, but only one Dorothy Coffee. But the truth is," I said to her, "Dorothy fit your physical description, but we have thousands of members in our church family who would have reached out to you the same way Dorothy did."

Some months ago, Dorothy Coffee died. She was ninety-four years old. I told this story at her memorial service. But let me ask you something: Where did Dorothy and the rest of us learn how to reach out to others like that? Where did we learn to run to greet people like that, to welcome people home like that, to love people into the family like that? You know, don't you? Of course you do; Dorothy and the rest of us learned that from Jesus. We learned that in Sunday school and in church. We learned it from the parable of the prodigal son because we learned in that story that God is gracious, and God wants us to be gracious too. In this great parable, Jesus taught us to love unconditionally, to love intentionally, to love compassionately, to love so enthusiastically that we make every person we meet feel as though we have put on them the best robe, the robe of the guest of honor.

That's number one—the robe of honor.

The Second of God's Great Gifts Is the Ring

In the first-century family, the ring was like "power of attorney." It was a signet ring with which you could make the official mark of the family. It gave you the authority to represent the family.

Talk about forgiveness! Talk about "amazing grace"! The father in this story demonstrates it dramatically. He gives his returning son the ring. After all that this son has done, and after all he has wasted, the father gives him the family ring, the privilege and authority to represent the family.

In the early days of the Salvation Army, it is said, a young man named Alexander was made treasurer of the Army. William Booth, the founder of the Salvation Army, and his wife, Catherine, loved Alexander. They trusted him and treated him like a son.

Little by little, however, Alexander began taking money from the treasury. He took more and more until finally he was caught and arrested and sent to jail. William and Catherine Booth still loved Alexander. They visited him in prison, wrote him letters weekly, and prayed for him daily.

Alexander was touched by their gracious spirit. He was penitent, and he asked for their forgiveness. On the morning Alexander was released from jail, Mrs. Booth was waiting outside the front gate of the prison with a canister of hot tea. She invited Alexander to sit down on a nearby bench, and then she poured him a cup of tea.

"Alexander," she said, "I have something here more than tea." She reached into her purse and pulled out a moneybag. "General Booth and I want you to come back to the Salvation

Army and help us," she said to him. "And we want you to begin your duties as treasurer this very morning."

Let me ask you something: Can *you* love like that? Can you forgive like that? That's what grace is. That's the way God loves and forgives us, and that's the way God wants us to love and forgive one another. That's what the gift of the ring means. It means that we have the power, the privilege, the authority, and the responsibility to represent God; or, if you put a hyphen in the word, to re-present God, to represent and re-present God and his family.

God gives to us, first, the robe of honor and, second, the ring of authority to represent him and his family. And God wants us to pass those great gifts on to others as we imitate his gracious spirit.

The Third Gift Is the Shoes

The father had a pair of sandals placed upon his returning son's feet. This gift of shoes meant that the prodigal son was still a member of the family. If you and I got in a time machine and went back to the first century and visited a farm, we likely would see children playing together, and immediately we would notice that some of those children had shoes while others were barefooted. The children with shoes would be the sons and daughters of the farmer, and those without shoes would be the children of the servants. Having shoes was an outward symbol that meant you were in the family. Remember the prodigal son's confession: "Father, I'm no longer worthy to be called your son. Treat me like one of your hired hands." But the father, with this gift of shoes, says, "No, you are still my son. You are a precious member of our family."

Last year, a young mother suddenly became critically ill. Her husband rushed her to the emergency room. The couple's two-year-old son, Jeff, stayed at his grandmother's house. The young mother, whose name was Amanda, was kept in the hospital for several days, and her husband stayed by her side.

Meanwhile, the grandmother had run into a problem with two-year-old Jeff. He refused to take his shoes off, even in bed. Jeff's grandmother would creep into his room at two o'clock in the morning to remove his shoes, and as soon as she would touch the shoes, Jeff would instantly wake up. Jeff's grandmother finally realized what was happening. She explained, "To [two-year-old] Jeff, keeping his shoes on meant that his mommy and daddy soon would be coming back to take him home."

That's pretty close to this first-century concept. Having shoes meant that "you belong; you are still in the family; you are not forgotten or rejected; you are a precious member of our family."

Some years ago, when I was on the staff of First United Methodist Church in Shreveport, I was sitting in Dr. D. L. Dykes's office one Monday morning. Suddenly, a young teenage girl appeared at the door, crying. She said she wanted to talk to both of us.

Through tears and sobs, she blurted out her story. She was in trouble. She was not married, was still in high school, and now was expecting a child. We comforted her and consoled her and encouraged her the best we could, and then she said, "I'm scared to tell my daddy. I want you to tell him for me."

Dr. Dykes wheeled his chair around and telephoned the girl's father, and he said some words I will never forget. He said, "Your daughter is here with Jim and me. We have something to tell you, and when we tell you, we are going to find out if you are worthy to be her father."

Well, it turned out that the girl's father was

worthy. He was a great father. He immediately came and put "shoes" on his daughter's feet. He and the girl's mother loved her through that difficult situation in a spirit of grace and compassion and family.

Do you know how they were able to do that? It was because they had learned from Jesus and from the parable of the prodigal son how to accept and give the robe of honor, the ring of authority and witness, and the shoes of love.

5

The Lost and Found Elder Brother

Scripture: Luke 15:25-32

Have you heard the story about a little girl named Mikki who was walking down the sidewalk with her mother one day? They were walking together, mom and daughter, holding hands.

As they walked along, little Mikki asked: "Mommy, what is God?" Her mother answered: "Well, Mikki, God is the creative force, the first cause, the unmoved mover, the unseen primal producer of existence, the binding, sentient energy that underpins all physical manifestation, the ..."

At this point, the little girl interrupted.

"Mommy, Mommy, wait! Use words that are my size. Tell me, Mommy, what is God?"

Mom took a deep breath and tried again, "Really, Mikki, it's hard to explain. God's like all the good stuff, the essence of all the beauty around us. God is ... well ... God is ..."

Mikki realized that her mom was struggling. She helped out by saying: "Mommy, I think God is love." Her mom smiled, hugged her, and said: "That just proves one thing, Mikki. You are smarter than most of the adults I know."

Mikki in her childlike way had simply, but profoundly, put her finger on the good news of our faith. God is love. God is our friend. God cares about each one of us. God is on our side. God will never desert us. We may run away from God or turn away from him, but God will always be there for us because—as Mikki put it so well—God is love!

That is what the first part of the parable of the prodigal son teaches us, that God is always anxious to love, quick to forgive, and eager to reconcile because God is like a gracious, patient, merciful, forgiving, loving parent.

The first part of the parable teaches us that God loves unconditionally. The second part of the parable, which focuses on the elder brother, teaches us that God wants us to love like that too. It teaches us that God wants us to love unconditionally, and yet we don't want to! In the first part of the parable, the prodigal son does everything wrong:

- He demands his inheritance early. How arrogant and presumptuous!
- He selfishly runs away to the far country.
- He squanders all of his money, one-third of the family's entire estate he fritters away in riotous living. (All kinds of sordid images come to mind.)

And then he hits bottom. With no money, he can't eat. The young man is so hungry that he takes a job as, of all things, a feeder of pigs. In Jewish culture in those days, this was the absolute "pits" because the pig was seen as the dramatic symbol of everything dirty and filthy and unclean. For a Jew in those days, nothing could be considered lower or more embarrassing than being a feeder of pigs.

But it is there in the pigsty that the prodigal son comes to his senses. He realizes how foolish and selfish and arrogant he has been. So in penitence and in shame, dirty and hungry, the picture of total defeat, he heads home.

The young man's father sees him coming,

and with joy and relief, the father runs to meet him, to hug him, to welcome him home, and to love him back into the family. The father then calls for a great party to celebrate the safe return of his son. Jesus told this great parable to show us what God is like and how God is always anxious to love, quick to forgive, and eager to reconcile.

Now, when I was a younger Christian, I used to wish this parable had ended here, with the party. I used to wish that somehow the second part about the elder brother had gotten lost. But over the years, I have come to realize and appreciate why it's here, and how very, very important it is.

The first part of the parable shows us that God is loving, and the second part of the parable shows us that God wants us to be loving like him. But we (like the elder brother) are reluctant to do that. God wants us to live in the spirit of unconditional love. God wants us to be anxious to love, quick to forgive, and eager to reconcile; but we (like the elder brother) are hesitant about doing that.

Dramatically, this parable shows us that when we live in that gracious, loving, forgiving spirit of the Father, life is a great celebration, a feast, a party. But when we (like the elder brother) turn away from that loving spirit, then we become likely prospects for a life of bitterness, misery, and loneliness.

Some years ago, I heard a beautiful story about a boy whose parents were missionaries to India. When the boy was twelve years old, his parents left him and his younger brother to go to India and take up their tour of duty there.

Their intention was that once they got settled, they would send for the boys. But shortly after they left America, World War II broke out. The parents couldn't get to the boys and they couldn't bring the boys to where they were. So the separation between the missionaries and their sons went on for something like eight years. Can you imagine what that was like?

When the war was over, the parents returned to America. Their older son was twenty years old and in college. He recalled how excited he was when he got the word that his parents would soon arrive in their hometown by train. The son got to the train depot early, even before the sun came up. When the train finally pulled in, the mother and father were the only ones who got off the train. The son later wrote these words:

> I could barely see them in the haze, and they could hardly see me. We embraced in the semi-darkness. Then, my mother took my hand and led me into the light of

the waiting room. There were tears running down her cheeks as she looked at me. She kept looking at my face, staring hard. Then she turned to my dad and called him by name, "Arnett," she cried, "He's gone and looked just like you! He looks just like you!"

That is what the parable of the prodigal son is teaching us: to "go and look like" our Father, to take on the loving and gracious characteristics of God, to love unconditionally like him.

I would like to think that there is a third part of the parable in which, later on in his life, the elder brother "gets it," but at this time, as the parable is told, he hasn't gotten it yet. At this point, he is not looking like his father at all. While the father is gracious and loving and forgiving, the elder brother is resentful and envious and judgmental.

Look with me now at these three hurtful, un-Godlike attitudes that prevent us from celebrating life.

First of All, the Elder Brother Was Resentful

There is nothing Godlike about resentment. In my opinion, there is nothing more destructive to our spirits than brooding, seething resentment. Resentment is a spiritual poison. It can ruin your life and devastate your soul.

This was happening to the elder brother in the story. He resented the homecoming his brother was receiving. He resented the generosity of his father. And he resented the work he had done for his father. Look at his words here. He says to the father: "For all these years I have been working like a slave for you" (Luke 15:29). Notice this now:

- The elder brother does not see his work as a wonderful opportunity.
- He does not see his work as a joyful thing to do alongside his father or brother.
- He does not see his work as a grateful response to his father's blessings graciously shared with him.
- No, he says, "I have been slaving away," and the words drip with the spirit of resentment.
- And in speaking to his father, who has come out graciously to invite him in to the party, the elder brother refers to his newly returned brother as "this son of yours" (Luke 15:30). Sounds almost like a curse, doesn't it? It's as if he is really saying, "This

son of yours is no brother of mine." The words drip with the spirit of resentment.

Resentment is a dangerous attitude because it can make you sick. It can hurt you and other people.

When I was a little boy, I loved the comedy of Abbott and Costello. Those of you who are over fifty years old grew up with this great comedy team. Those of you under the age of fifty are probably still familiar with their classic "Who's On First?" routine.

One night on their radio program years ago, Lou Costello was wearing a beautiful flower in his lapel. Throughout the program, people kept complimenting his lapel flower, much to Lou Costello's delight. But then a neighbor named Scotty came along, admired the flower, and then suddenly, without warning, he pulled Lou Costello's flower out of his lapel and put it on himself and walked away whistling.

Why, this made Lou Costello so angry. And as the radio program went on, he became more and more angry, more and more resentful toward Scotty for taking his flower.

Finally, Lou Costello said to Bud Abbott, "I'm ready for Scotty now. Just let him try to take my flower out of my lapel now, and see what he gets!"

"What have you done, Lou?" asked Bud Abbott.

Lou Costello answered proudly, "I have put a hand grenade in my coat pocket, and I have tied the flower to the pin of the hand grenade, so when Scotty takes my flower *this* time it's gonna blow his hand clean off. That'll teach him!" But, you see, what Lou Costello didn't realize was that at the same time, the hand grenade would blow his own heart right out!

That's the way resentment works, and there is nothing Godlike about it. Jesus knew that, and that is the reason he came to teach love and mercy and forgiveness and compassion. That's why in this parable and in his other teachings Jesus showed us that God is loving and that God wants us to live in that spirit. God wants us to be loving like him.

First of all, the elder brother missed the party because he was resentful.

Second, the Elder Brother Missed the Party Because He Was Envious

Envy is so deceptive and sneaky. It doesn't seem so bad, but let me tell you, it is lethal. And there is nothing Godlike about it.

I am thinking of a man I know in another state who has an excellent tenor voice. He is an outstanding singer, but he has not sung in church for more than thirty years.

Thirty-three years ago, this man was active in his church's music program, sang in the choir, and was the church's main soloist. People praised him often for his great talent. And all was beautiful, until a new singer moved to town and joined the choir.

The choir director asked the new man to sing a tenor solo one morning, and he was magnificent! When the main soloist heard the new man sing, he recognized that this new singer had gifts far superior to his own. And when he heard how the people thanked the new man and complimented him, the main soloist could not stand it. Something happened within him. He knew he could not sing as well as the new man, and envy moved into his spirit. It consumed and ruined his life.

He dropped out of the church and out of the choir, and he has sulked for thirty-three years. He rarely comes to church anymore, and when he does, he sits in the congregation with bitterness written all over his face. He is mad most of the time: He is cynical and critical of the church, especially the music program; but people long ago stopped listening to him.

Here is a man who has wasted his talent and who has wasted thirty-three years. Think of what he has missed while making himself miserable through pettiness and jealousy and envy.

Jesus knew how destructive envy can be. That's why he encouraged us to be loving and gracious and big-spirited like God, not resentful and not envious.

Third and Finally, the Elder Brother Missed the Party Because He Was Judgmental

I have noticed something over the years. I have noticed that the great people of faith I have known—the ones who really inspired me—were not harsh, critical, judgmental people. No, the ones who touched my heart and inspired me so much were the ones who just seemed to become more and more loving with each passing day. They never said bad things about other people; they never acted "holier-than-thou." No, they were grateful, tender, caring, compassionate, merciful people. They were Godlike people who had received God's amazing grace and who then spent their days passing that gracious spirit on to others.

Isn't it sad that so many people miss that? Like the elder brother, they live in the presence of the Father, but somehow they miss his gracious, loving spirit.

In 1988, the poet Carol Wimmer became concerned about the self-righteous, judgmental spirit she was seeing in some people because she felt strongly that being judgmental is a perversion of the Christian faith. So, she wrote a poem about this. It's called "When I Say I Am a Christian," and it reads like this:

> When I say, "I am a Christian," I'm not shouting, "I've been saved!"
> I'm whispering, "I get lost! That's why I chose this way"
>
> When I say, "I am a Christian," I don't speak with human pride.
> I'm confessing that I stumble—needing God to be my guide
>
> When I say, "I am a Christian," I'm not trying to be strong.
> I'm professing that I'm weak and pray for strength to carry on
>
> When I say, "I am a Christian," I'm not bragging of success
> I'm admitting that I've failed and cannot ever pay the debt
>
> When I say, "I am a Christian," I don't think I know it all

I submit to my confusion asking humbly
to be taught

When I say, "I am a Christian," I'm not
claiming to be perfect
My flaws are far too visible but God
believes I'm worth it

When I say, "I am a Christian," I still feel
the sting of pain
I have my share of heartache which is why
I seek His name

When I say, "I am a Christian," I do not
wish to judge
I have no authority—I only know I'm loved

Now, if Jesus based this parable in Luke 15 on a
true story, we can only hope that eventually the
elder brother came to his senses and left the "far
country" of resentment and envy and self-
righteous judgment and came home. And if he did,
we can be sure of one thing: the Father ran to meet
him with open arms! Because our heavenly Father
is always anxious to love, quick to forgive, and
eager to reconcile. He wants *us* to be like that too!

6
The Lost and Found Celebration

Scripture: Luke 14:15-24

There is a fascinating story that comes out of World War II. United States President Franklin D. Roosevelt, Great Britain's Prime Minister Winston Churchill, and Soviet Union Premier Joseph Stalin met together at the Teheran Conference in late 1943 to shape a common policy to work together to win the war.

The discussion went well, and the three great nations for the most part reached cordial agreement on their strategy to end the war and to create a lasting peace. However, there was one point that Roosevelt and Churchill could not get Stalin to agree to or even consider. When cornered to give his reasons for not being willing to go along with this decision, Stalin responded by telling an ancient Arabian fable.

The fable was about a man who was approached one day by a neighbor who asked to borrow his rope. The man answered, "I can't lend you my rope because I must use it to tie up some milk."

The neighbor said, "What are you talking about? You can't tie up milk with a rope."

To which the man answered, "My friend, when you don't want to do something, one excuse is as good as another."

Excuse-making—that's what this parable in Luke 14 is all about. Jesus told the parable about a man who was giving a big dinner party and had sent out many invitations. When all was ready, the man sent out a servant to tell the invited guests, "Please come now, everything is ready."

Now at this point in the parable, we run across one of the most haunting verses in all of the Bible: "They all alike began to make excuses" (Luke 14:18). And as we read on, the parable tells us that these people all missed the party because of their excuse-making.

How relevant this parable is for us in our

time! We have become master excuse-makers. I'm sure that you have noticed it. How could you miss it? We are living in very frank times when nothing is kept under wraps anymore. People will admit to almost anything.

We see people on national television,

- laughing at their many marriage failures,
- admitting that they are living together without being married,
- having children out of wedlock,
- openly telling of their use of drugs and alcohol.

And, are you ready for this, the audience laughs and applauds!

Our problem, though, is not that we hesitate to admit anything, but rather our problem is that we are learning how to justify everything! We are quite adept at excuse-making.

Let me show you what I mean.

First, We Excuse Ourselves with Words— Well-chosen Words

Take, for example, the matter of *missing church*. Over the years, I have heard some great excuses for failure to make it to church. Some people blame the weather. Others blame it on having company. Still others blame their clothing.

One woman fascinated me with her excuse. In the five years I was pastor at her church, she never made it to church. It seemed that I was always running into her in crowded basketball arenas or in crowded theaters or at crowded parties, and she would always say, "Oh, Jim, I do wish I could come to church, but I can't stand to be in a crowd." I'm *still* trying to figure that one out!

However, my favorite excuse was given to me by a woman who said, "I don't go to church, and this is my reason: If I go *some* of the time, it makes me want to go *all* the time. And since I can't go *all* the time, it makes me feel guilty when I miss *some* of the time. So I don't go *any* of the time, and this keeps me from feeling guilty and wanting to go *all* the time." Now, *that*'s a real excuse, isn't it?

Or take the matter of *stealing*. I once heard a young man who had been arrested for shoplifting say, "I don't steal, I *obtain*. The store owners overcharge, so I am justified in *obtaining* some of the merchandise. It's all part of the game."

Or how about the young boy who took

money out of his own father's cash register and then excused himself by saying, "It wasn't my fault; he made me mad!"

Then there is *profanity,* which we try to justify by calling it mature, adult, honest, plain-spoken, realistic speech. Come on, now, what could be more immature, childish, dishonest, or unreal?

And what about *unfaithfulness*? This is the most universally justified and amazingly excused sin in the world. All the way from the classic "my wife doesn't understand me" to "if you love somebody, why isn't it all right?" Why, it has even been called (of all things) the "new morality." We call it the "new morality" and dupe ourselves because it is the oldest idolatry in the world.

Take the matter of *gossip*. Gossip is so dangerous, so cruel, so hurtful, so devastating, so sinful, and yet we indulge in it so frequently and excuse it so lightly. I once heard a man excuse his gossip by saying, "I won't tell anything about another person unless it is good, and, boy, is this good!"

Then, there is *temper*. Have you ever heard someone say something like this: "Oh, everybody knows I was born with a hot temper, but my temper is like a cyclone. It blows up quickly and just as quickly blows away." What people with a bad temper don't realize is this: Their temper may rise quickly like a cyclone, and it may pass quickly like a cyclone. But also, like a cyclone, it leaves behind immeasurable hurt and agony and heartache and devastation.

And what about *vengeance*? Over and over in the Gospels, Jesus warns us about the sin of the vengeful spirit. It's a spiritual poison that will destroy your soul. Jesus taught that emphatically. "Don't give in to vengeance," he said, and yet we justify it so eloquently and excuse it so neatly.

Remember how *All in the Family* TV character Archie Bunker put it: "What's wrong with revenge? It's the perfect way to get even." Or, remember the two little boys who got into a fight at recess. The teacher broke it up and one little boy said, "He started it when he hit me back!"

That's the first thing we do, we excuse ourselves with words—with well-chosen words.

Second, We Also Excuse Ourselves with the Use of Scapegoats

Oh, how we like to put the blame on someone else! This ploy is as old as the Garden of

Eden. Adam points at Eve and Eve points at the serpent. The cry here is, "It's not my fault," and the symbol is "the pointing finger." Think of how we use scapegoats to assuage our guilt.

We excuse ourselves by *blaming other people*. We learn this tactic early. When our son, Jeff, was six years old, he ran through the kitchen one Saturday morning and karate-chopped the dishwasher, accidentally hitting the *On* button. When the dishwasher started up, Jeff stopped in his tracks. He knew he had done something he shouldn't have done, but he quickly rose to the occasion. He said: "It's okay, Dad, we'll tell Mom *you* did it!"

We excuse ourselves by *blaming circumstances or past events*. I once knew a man who couldn't hold a job. We got him three different jobs. He would work for a day or two and then quit. Finally, I asked him why. He said, "It's all because of the food poisoning." "When did you get food poisoning?" I asked. He said, "The spring of 1947."

We excuse ourselves by *blaming evil spirits*. Comedian Flip Wilson's catchphrase, "The devil made me do it," can cover a multitude of sins. The idea here is that our behaviors can be controlled by demons. "I'm not responsible," we say, "the devil got into me."

I saw a cartoon on this notion recently. A

woman had bought a new dress that was very expensive. Her husband asked why she had been so extravagant. She replied, "The devil made me do it." "Well," the husband asked, "why didn't you say 'Get thee behind me, Satan'?" "I did," explained the wife, "but he said it looked as good in back as it did in front so I bought it."

This is a light comic treatment of a very serious subject. Ever since the book and movie *The Exorcist* came out years ago, I have been asked if I believe we are the helpless victims of evil spirits. My answer to that is an emphatic *no.* I do not believe God, our Father, would subject us to anything that would leave us powerless or cut us off from the abundant life Jesus came to share with us.

We have free will, freedom to choose. The truth is sometimes we choose poorly. Then we try to cover with excuses and scapegoats.

Third and Finally, What Does the Christian Faith Say to Us About Our Excuse-making?

Observation Number One: God sees through our excuses. Like a father who knows his children well, God knows us. God can't be "conned!" He knows us better than we know ourselves. He sees through us and our excuses. Our excuses seem so frail and feeble under the light of God.

That is what this strange little parable in Luke 14 is about. A man is giving a great banquet. The invitation goes out, "Come! All is ready!" Then there is that haunting line, "They all alike began to make excuses." The farmer says, "I have bought a field. I have business responsibilities. I pray you have me excused." The cattleman says, "I have bought five yoke of oxen. I must go examine them. I pray you have me excused." The married man says, "I have married a wife, and therefore I cannot come." Note the play on male humor here. The farmer and the cattlemen politely asked to be excused, but the married man says in effect, "You know I can't come, I'm a married man." (He took it like a man; he blamed it on his wife.) So the party is held without them.

The story has some strange elements, but there is one central truth here that we need to notice now, namely this: We can make excuses for almost anything we want to do or don't want to do, but God sees through them. And our excuses may be the very thing keeping us out of the kingdom of God. Our excuses may well be the very thing keeping us out of God's presence.

Observation Number Two: God is not so much interested in hearing our excuses as forgiving our sins. We don't need a scapegoat; we have a Savior. Christ came to show us that forgiveness is at hand. We see it powerfully in the parable of the prodigal son, which we read in Luke 15 and examined in previous chapters.

The prodigal son comes home, rehearsing his confessions all the way. When he comes face to face with the father, he begins to blurt it out. But look: (don't miss this!) The father interrupts him. He doesn't want to hear it. He wants to get on with the celebration. Forgiveness was there, available all along. The prodigal had only to come back and accept it.

No more talk needed. No excuses necessary. "Bring the best robe and put it on him; put a ring on his hand and shoes on his feet. Let's have a feast, for this, my son, was dead and now he is alive again; he was lost, but now is found."

Here's the point: *We are not justified by our eloquent excuses, but by the grace of a loving, caring, forgiving Father!*

Observation Number Three: What God wants is not excuses, but penitence. What is said with the lips is not nearly so important as what happens in the heart. We see this dramatically in Jesus' parable of the Pharisee and the publican (a tax collector), who go up to the Temple to pray in Luke 18:9-14.

The Pharisee tries to "excuse" himself. He tries to cover his guilt with words. "Lord, I do this, I do that! See how righteous I am!" Then, he tries scapegoats. "Lord, I thank you that I'm not like other men, and especially this publican." On and on the Pharisee goes with words, excuses, cover-ups, scapegoats. But then there is the publican, with his prayer of penitence. He bows his head humbly, beats upon his chest, and cries, "God, be merciful to me, a sinner!"

Then the parable closes with this: "I tell you, this man [the publican] went down to his home justified rather than the other [the Pharisee]" (Luke 18:14*a*). What God wants is not excuses, but penitence.

When I was on the staff at First United Methodist Church in Shreveport, I learned many things from Dr. D. L. Dykes. Let me tell you about one of those learning experiences.

One of our secretaries came to my office in tears one morning. She said a woman had just called who was very upset. This woman had been in the hospital for a few days, and no one from the church had visited her. She felt neglected. She was hurt and angry and had told the secretary so, in no uncertain terms.

I told the secretary that I would go out to see this woman right away. As I was leaving, I ran into D. L. in the office area. I told him the situation, and he said, "I'll go with you."

As we drove out to the hospital, I began to think about facing this irate woman, and I began to put together some good excuses. By the time we got there, I had a pretty good list.

When we went into the hospital room, the woman turned on us and set us straight; she berated us and told us off. Just as I was about to defend us with my "ready-made excuses," D. L. spoke up first and said to her, "You are absolutely right. We have neglected you. It is inexcusable. We are so sorry we failed you, and we want so much to make it up to you right now. We want to do better. Can you find it in your heart to forgive us?"

She did! She smiled. She said, "I didn't mean to be so harsh. It's just that I was hurt and I'm so lonely." We joined hands and made a circle of love there. We had a prayer together and became reconciled.

As we walked out of that hospital room I realized that D. L. was right. It's not excuses that matter, it's penitence!

The parable of the banquet in Luke 14 reminds us that

- God sees through our feeble excuses,
- God is more interested in forgiving our sins than in hearing our excuses, and
- what God wants from us is not excuses, but penitence.

The hymn-writer put it like this:

Amazing grace! How sweet the sound
That saved a wretch like me!
I once was lost, but now am found;
Was blind, but now I see.
(John Newton, "Amazing Grace," 1779)

SUGGESTIONS FOR LEADING A STUDY OF *JESUS' PARABLES OF THE LOST AND FOUND*

John D. Schroeder

This book by James W. Moore examines the lost-and-found aspects of some of the parables told by Jesus and applies their lessons to life today. To assist you in facilitating a discussion group, this study guide was created to help make this experience beneficial for both you and members of your group. Here are some thoughts on how you can help your group:

1. Distribute the book to participants before your first meeting and request that they come having read the brief introduction and the first

chapter. You may want to limit the size of your group to increase participation.

2. Begin your sessions on time. Your participants will appreciate your promptness. You may wish to begin your first session with introductions and a brief get-acquainted time. Start each session by reading aloud the snapshot summary of the chapter for the day.

3. Select discussion questions and activities in advance. Note that the first question is a general question designed to get discussion going. The last question is designed to summarize the discussion. Feel free to change the order of the listed questions and to create your own questions. Allow a set amount of time for the questions and activities.

4. Remind your participants that all questions are valid as part of the learning process. Encourage their participation in discussion by saying that there are no "wrong" answers and that all input will be appreciated. Invite participants to share their thoughts, personal stories, and ideas as their comfort level allows.

5. Some questions may be more difficult to answer than others. If you ask a question and no one responds, begin the discussion by venturing an answer yourself. Then ask for comments and other answers. Remember that some questions may have multiple answers.

6. Ask the question "Why?" or "Why do you believe that?" to help continue a discussion and give it greater depth.

7. Give everyone a chance to talk. Keep the conversation moving. Occasionally you may want to direct a question to a specific person who has been quiet. "Do you have anything to add?" is a good follow-up question to ask another person. If the topic of conversation gets off track, move ahead by asking the next question in your study guide.

8. Before moving from questions to activities, ask group members if they have any questions that have not been answered. Remember that as a leader, you do not have to know all the answers. Some answers may come from group members. Other answers may even need a bit of research. Your job is to keep the discussion moving and to encourage participation.

9. Review the activity in advance. Feel free to modify it or to create your own activity. Encourage participants to try the "At home" activity.

10. Following the conclusion of the activity, close with a brief prayer, praying either the printed prayer from the study guide or a prayer of your own. If your group desires, pause for individual prayer petitions.

11. Be grateful and supportive. Thank group members for their ideas and participation.

12. You are not expected to be a "perfect" leader. Just do the best you can by focusing on the participants and the lesson. God will help you lead this group.

13. Enjoy your time together!

Suggestions for Participants

1. What you will receive from this study will be in direct proportion to your involvement. Be an active participant!

2. Please make it a point to attend all sessions and to arrive on time so that you can receive the greatest benefit.

3. Read the chapter and review the study guide questions prior to the meeting. You may want to jot down questions you have from the reading and also answers to some of the study guide questions.

4. Be supportive and appreciative of your group leader as well as of the other members of your group. You are on a journey together.

5. Your participation is encouraged. Feel free to share your thoughts about the material being discussed.

6. Pray for your group and your leader.

Chapter 1
The Lost and Found Sheep

Snapshot Summary

This chapter reminds us that God's love is inclusive, forgiving, and sacrificial and that God wants us to love others the same way.

Reflection / Discussion Questions

1. How does this parable speak to you? How is it relevant to your life today? Share why you selected this book to read and what you hope to learn from it.

2. List some reasons why people become lost and drift away from the church and from God.

3. Share a time when you were shown compassion or were compassionate.

4. Reflect on / discuss what it means for us that God's love is inclusive.

5. List some practical ways that we can be inclusive in our loving.

6. Name some "curtains" that separate and divide people today.

7. Discuss what it means to forgive someone.

8. What sometimes prevents us from forgiving others?

9. How does it feel to be forgiven? Give an example.

10. Share a lesson you learned about sacrifice as a child or as an adult.

11. What makes us sometimes reluctant to sacrifice?

12. Reflect on / discuss how Jesus' life exemplified what a good shepherd should be.

Activities

As a group: Create a design for a car bumper sticker that conveys a lost-and-found lesson from this chapter or from your group discussion.

At home: Reflect on whether you are a lost or a found sheep.

Prayer: *Dear God, thank you for your love that is inclusive, forgiving, and sacrificial. Help us follow your example and love others as you love us. May we be good shepherds to all who need our help and care. In Jesus' name. Amen.*

Chapter 2
The Lost and Found Coin

Snapshot Summary

This chapter reminds us of the responsibility we have for our children, for our church, and for our friends.

Reflection / Discussion Questions

1. Share a time when you searched for something you lost.

2. What are your thoughts about the story of the Doctor and the Reverend?

3. What are some of the reasons the author mentioned that the woman in the parable may have been frantic to find her lost coin?

4. If you lost something very valuable, how would you feel, and what actions would you take?

5. How is this parable similar to the parable of the lost sheep?

6. Reflect on / discuss how children are of high value.

7. How do children get "lost," and how can this be prevented?

8. What is the best gift you can give children, and why?

9. List some of the responsibilities that Christians have for the church.

10. Name some ways people get "lost" within or apart from the church.

11. List some warning signs that a friend may be "lost" and in need of your help.

12. Reflect on / discuss how people can tell we are Christians. How are Christians identified?

Activities

As a group: Your group is forming a Search and Rescue Squad for lost souls. List some of the equipment you will need and the places you will search.

At home: Take action this week to help a child, to serve the church, or to assist a friend in need.

Prayer: *Dear God, thank you for children, for the church, and for friends. They mean so much to us. Help us be responsive to their needs. Open our eyes to see the lost and those in danger of becoming lost. Help us act with wisdom and courage to take on the challenges we see around us. Amen.*

Chapter 3
The Lost and Found Son

Snapshot Summary

This chapter looks at the traits and character of the prodigal son, the elder brother, and the father in this parable.

Reflection / Discussion Questions

1. What makes the parable of the prodigal son so powerful?

2. What circumstances might lead to a feeling of uncertainty about returning home?

3. How does it feel to return home after an absence? How do you believe the younger son in the parable felt upon his return?

4. How are we sometimes like the prodigal son? What traits do we have in common with him?

5. What was the sin of the prodigal son?

6. What choices did the father in the parable have about how to respond?

7. What adjectives describe the elder brother?

8. What made the elder brother so angry? Is it easy to identify with his anger? Why or why not?

9. How were the older and younger brothers alike?

10. Explain why the faher is the real hero and focus of this parable.

11. What does this parable tell us God is like?

12. What additional points or lessons did Jesus want to make by telling this story?

Activities

As a group: Let each group member create an invitation to a party for the prodigal son as written by the father. Share your creations.

At home: Reflect on the goodness of God, our Father.

Prayer: *Dear God, thank you for giving us this great parable and for all the life lessons contained within it. Help us take these lessons to heart and apply them in our lives. Amen.*

Chapter 4
The Lost and Found Gifts

Snapshot Summary

This chapter looks at the great gifts that God has reserved for us—the robe of honor, the ring of authority and witness, and the shoes of love.

Reflection / Discussion Questions

1. What makes a gift a great gift?

2. Share a time when you gave a special gift to someone. How did you select it, and how did it make you feel to give it?

3. Share a time when you were the recipient of a special gift. How did receiving this gift make you feel?

4. For the members of Jesus' first-century audience, what was the unexpected surprise within this parable?

5. What does it mean to be gracious? Give an example.

6. What does this parable tell us about how God loves and how God wants us to love?

7. What do we have to do to be a recipient of the gifts of God?

8. What does the father's gift of the ring mean or signify in this parable?

9. Share a time when you were given "shoes" of love by someone.

10. Reflect on / discuss what it means to give others a robe of honor.

11. Why do we give gifts to others? List some of the reasons why and the different types of gifts we can give.

12. What does it mean to be a "worthy"

father or mother (or son, daughter, spouse, sibling, and so forth)?

Activities

As a group: Let each group member create a gift certificate for a thoughtful service that he or she will perform for someone this coming week. Share your ideas. (These may include kind words, kind deeds, and so forth.)

At home: Take an inventory of your gifts this week—those you have available to give and those you have received.

Prayer: *Dear God, thank you for the special gifts you give us each and every day. Help us not take these gifts for granted but share the treasure you give us with others. Show us how to be joyful givers. Amen.*

Chapter 5
The Lost and Found Elder Brother

Snapshot Summary

This chapter examines the attitudes that prevent us from celebrating life, such as resentment, envy, and being judgmental.

Reflection / Discussion Questions

1. "God is love"; reflect on / discuss the meaning of this truth.

2. List some of the common barriers to loving others.

3. What is envy, and why is it harmful?

4. Share a time when, either as a child or as an adult, you were resentful.

5. Name a person you know who is an example of love in action. Briefly describe this person.

6. List reasons why the elder brother was resentful. Were any of his reasons justified?

7. If you feel envious, what action should you take?

8. Share a time when you acted like the elder brother.

9. Explain what difference there is, if any, between envy and resentment. (Consider using a dictionary to compare definitions.) How are the two related?

10. What makes a person critical and judgmental?

11. How can love from God and love from others change us?

12. Which of the three traits (envy, resentment, and being judgmental) do you believe is the worst, and why?

Activities

As a group: Create your own set of statements about what it means to you to call yourself a Christian—what you personally mean or what you are professing when you say that—and share them with the group.

At home: Reflect upon what roles envy, resentment, and being judgmental play in your life, and think about how these roles can be reduced or eliminated.

Prayer: *Dear God, thank you for giving us the power to overcome envy, resentment, and being critical of others. Open our eyes to see how these attitudes poison us and prevent us from celebrating life. Help us love others the way that you love us. Amen.*

Chapter 6
The Lost and Found Celebration

Snapshot Summary

This chapter looks at the words and scapegoats we use to make excuses for ourselves and how God views our words and deeds.

Reflection / Discussion Questions

1. What's the difference between a good (valid) excuse and a bad excuse?

2. Reflect on / discuss what motivates people to make excuses.

3. Do you agree with the author that we are learning to justify everything? Explain your response.

4. List some valid reasons for and some invalid reasons for not attending worship services at church.

5. In what ways do we make excuses to God?

6. How does God view excuse-making?

7. What do we learn about excuses from this parable?

8. Reflect on / discuss the role that justification and blame play in making excuses.

9. How do you feel, and what do you think, when you receive an excuse from someone else? Compare this with how you feel when you give an excuse.

10. Reflect on / discuss some alternatives to making excuses.

11. What are scapegoats? Explain why we, with God, do not need scapegoats.

12. How have your reading and discussions of this book helped or challenged you?

Activities

As a group: Have a group celebration and graduation party to signify the completion of reading and discussing this book. Create, sign, and share graduation diplomas.

At home: Reflect on and make a list of what you have learned from your experience with this book.

Prayer: *Dear God, thank you for all of the goodness you pack into our lives. Help us not make excuses, but join the celebration, and love others as you love us. Amen .*